KETTLEBELL

Day Plan to Burning Fat, Packing on Muscle and Getting Ripped

(Kettlebell Workouts for Building Massive Muscles)

William Pettry

Published by Tomas Edwards

© **William Pettry**

All Rights Reserved

Kettlebell: Day Plan to Burning Fat, Packing on Muscle and Getting Ripped (Kettlebell Workouts for Building Massive Muscles)

ISBN 978-1-990268-62-5

All rights reserved. No part of this guide may be reproduced in any form without permission in writing from the publisher except in the case of brief quotations embodied in critical articles or reviews.

Legal & Disclaimer

The information contained in this book is not designed to replace or take the place of any form of medicine or professional medical advice. The information in this book has been provided for educational and entertainment purposes only.

The information contained in this book has been compiled from sources deemed reliable, and it is accurate to the best of the Author's knowledge; however, the Author cannot guarantee its accuracy and validity and cannot be held liable for any errors or omissions. Changes are periodically made to this book. You must consult your doctor or get professional medical advice before using any of the suggested remedies, techniques, or information in this book.

Upon using the information contained in this book, you agree to hold harmless the Author from and against any damages, costs, and expenses, including any legal fees potentially resulting from the application of any of the information provided by this guide. This disclaimer applies to any damages or injury caused by the use and application, whether directly or indirectly, of any advice or information presented, whether for breach of contract, tort, negligence, personal injury, criminal intent, or under any other cause of action.

You agree to accept all risks of using the information presented inside this book. You need to consult a professional medical practitioner in order to ensure you are both able and healthy enough to participate in this program.

Table of Contents

INTRODUCTION 1

CHAPTER 1: BENEFITS OF KETTLEBELLS 8

CHAPTER 2: HOW HEAVY SHOULD YOU LIFT? 14

CHAPTER 3: THE KETTLEBELL AND CROSSFIT TRAINING ... 26

CHAPTER 4: BIG MUSCLES AND KETTLEBELLS 30

CHAPTER 5: TIPS TO GET AN EDGE IN TRAINING 34

CHAPTER 6: KETTLEBELL WORKOUTS FOR BEGINNERS 48

CHAPTER 7: ADVANCED EXERCISES 72

CHAPTER 8: STRETCHING OUT AND WARMING UP 78

CHAPTER 9: OPTIMIZED SOVIET KETTLEBELL ROUTINES .. 86

CHAPTER 10: KETTLEBELL FAT LOSS WORKOUT 95

CHAPTER 11: BEGINNER KETTLEBELL WORKOUTS. 109

CHAPTER 12: BEGINNERS, INTERMEDIATE AND ADVANCED LEVEL KETTLEBELL WORKOUT PLAN 118

CONCLUSION 130

Introduction

A very fitting quote by one of the most mentally and physically tough individuals in history. Working out and getting in tremendous shape can be torturous at times, however, the results are often worth it. I will admit though, the above quote is a little misleading, despite how much I may enjoy it, and even lived it. Working out, training, and getting in shape can be difficult, taxing, and a little painful. In fact, it will be all of those things. If it isn't, you are not pushing yourself enough.

Change is never easy and if you are actively trying to grow for the better, it is not always going to be sunshine and rainbows. It is going to take a lot of hard work, but the last time I checked, hard is not a synonym for bad. On the contrary, the harder something is, the more fun it can actually be. That being said, working out hard and getting in shape is not something you have to hate. Many people attribute the mindset of wanting to look good to women. This includes the self-consciousness that comes with not living up to society's standards when it comes to personal appearance. Many women feel that they don't measure up and never will because they can't see their own beauty due to always comparing themselves to others. However, this way of thinking is not exclusive to women. Many men out there are also very self-conscious about how they look. They care about having that six-pack and also looking good in that new t-shirt, just like women do. Which gender is more concerned about personal appearance is a topic for another day. For now, we want to instill the fact that men care about looking good too. They care about getting in shape and burning excess fat.

For many males out there, this can be difficult. They have tried various different workouts, both traditional and nontraditional, and never come close to the results they want to see. This becomes more of an issue as we age. This is quite frustrating indeed. Most men are not looking to become the next Dwayne "The Rock" Johnson or Mark Wahlberg. They are trying to get in shape, look good, and feel healthy through exercises that are efficient and fun. However, there is so much to choose from and so much exercise equipment available that may or may not work. Well, I have something for you.

There is an old-school, simple to use and understand piece of equipment that allows for a variety of workouts. These exercises are challenging, fun, and can be done almost anywhere. What we are referring to here is the kettlebell. If you hate going to the gym, no problem because the kettlebell will be there for you. Do you love going to the gym? That's fine too, because they will likely have some kettlebells you can use. This piece of equipment may seem like a glorified dumbbell to some, but as you will all see, it is so much more than that. It is like the Swiss army knife of exercise equipment because of all the functions it serves in the training realm.

By the time you complete this book, you will understand everything you need to know about kettlebells, including numerous exercises that will work out many different areas of the body. After that, it will be all up to you to make things happen. Because after all, knowledge is power, but the action is what creates results. While we will be getting very in-depth through the various chapters of this book, I want to touch on some high points to get all of you excited. Here are some major benefits of the kettlebell to get things started.

Kettlebell workouts are very effective at burning fat. When done properly, these routines can burn up to 400 calories in a single 20-minute session. The combination of intensity and targeting of specific areas on the body makes for impeccable results, even for hard to reach places. This will be a major time saver for all of your busy-bodies out there.

Multiple clinical studies have shown that various workouts with this equipment can and will increase strength and power. You can also improve your conditioning in a major way. One of the best things is, movements using the kettlebell often mimic natural body movements, allowing for ease when transitioning into the workouts.

With many different pieces of equipment out there, you are targeting one muscle or area of the body. With the kettlebell, you are targeting multiple areas while placing different demands simultaneously in these areas. So if two muscles are being activated at the same time, they will feel a different intensity level based on the routine. Dumbbells, for example, can provide great workouts, but the physical nature of them causes many limitations.

Kettlebell exercises can work out almost any area of the body and really targets your core. You will notice major core conditioning as you start the various exercises.

Not only will the kettlebell help you feel and look better, but it will provide immense health benefits. Cardiovascular health is one of the major benefits. The immense calorie burn is equivalent to running a six-minute mile. Furthermore, the kettlebell can provide for great back exercises and improve its health and function, especially when it comes to posture. Finally, this diverse piece of equipment can be used for many rehabilitative purposes. Many rehab specialists, including physical therapists, utilize the kettlebell for their various workouts. This goes along the lines of kettlebell training mimicking natural movements.

All of these benefits are just the tips of the iceberg. As we go through this book, we will detail exactly what the kettlebell is, the different forms it comes in, the history behind it, detailed kettlebell training, different exercises that can be utilized, and many other essentials to make your experience with this tool amazing. We will help you determine what is best for you and figure out a way for you to bring this tool into your life. Just like with any other product, safety concerns will play a role. Throughout this book, keeping ourselves free from injury will be a common theme. The last thing I want is for you to get injured by doing something wrong.

Chapter 1: Benefits Of Kettlebells

I thought I would briefly go over some of the great benefits that you can expect once you stat performing your kettlebell workouts. These are just SOME of the benefits, there are certain more, but these are the basic ones that I thought it would be appropriate to mention.

More Fun Than Regular Workouts – In my opinion kettlebell workouts are easily the least boring workout that I have other done. I think it's a tie between kettlebell workouts and jump rope workouts, but anyway I usually have more fun performing exercises with kettlebells. Most of my life I have been working out with the typical weights like dumbbells and barbells. I like to change it up a lot in order to stay focused and more engaged. If I were to the same workout, with the same weights every week then I would really hate the whole experience. That's why I love kettlebell workouts.

Strength endurance – Kettlebell workouts are great for improving your strength endurance. This basically means your ability to perform fast explosive movements when your body is close to or at anaerobic levels. (See the reference section to learn more about anaerobic and how it's different than aerobic.) This is why so many athletes and people who participate in fighting sports use kettlebells in their workouts. You will learn that a lot of kettlebell exercises involve you to force the weight in fast motions, which is why your strength endurance is so much affected.

Strong grip – You will notice as you perform your weekly kettlebell workouts that your hands will become a lot stronger. Your grip may be may weak at first, especially when you are use a heavy kettlebell, but once you start doing the exercises regularly, you will be able to grip them a lot easier. This can also be done performing other exercises that involve dumbbells, but you get much more out of the exercises using heavy kettlebells. I think it's really important to have strong hands because this will allow you to perform exercises with heavier weight.

Strength and cardio – One befit that I think is why kettlebells are so popular is because they combine a great strength workout, as well as a great cardio workout as well. Both having the ability to increase your strength and at the same time getting your heart rate up and really useful if you don't have enough time to workout for long periods. Kettlebells enable you to perform really quick workouts and still achieve the same results (or better) as compared to regular workouts.

Fat Loss – Because kettlebell workouts help speed up your heart rate and it's ability to help speed up your metabolic rate, naturally kettlebell workouts are great for losing excess fat. And the best part is that you really don't have to perform intricate exercises or workouts to make this happen. You usually will only have to perform one exercise if you want, to achieve some amazing fat loss results. (Take a look at the case study in the resources section to learn more about fat loss and how simple it is to do it using kettlebells.)

Stimulates Muscle Growth – I'm pretty sure that this point doesn't need that much explaining. What do you think is going to happen you start hurling around a heavy "rock" with a handle on it? But needless to say kettlebells will definitely stimulate your muscles and you can potential pack some great muscle mass. Although some kettlebell exercises may be better than others because of the difference between their time under tension (TUT). The more TUT, using heavy weights, and involving explosive exercises will dramatically increase your testosterone levels and kettlebells are good for doing all three of these things.

Posture – This point is interesting. Performing kettlebell workouts on a regular basis will help improve your posture by improving your posture chain.

This basically means the muscles that run along your backside, from neck to your feet. By strengthen them and involving movements from kettlebell exercises you will be able to stand up more straight.

Flexibility – Kettlebell exercises are good for help increasing your flexibly in your hip flexors, hamstrings, hip abductors, and any other areas of your body. The movements that you will be doing in your kettlebell workouts will increase your range of motion and as you progress, you will notice an improvement in bending in ways you probably may never have before.

More Coordination – The more exposed you get to kettlebells that better your coordination will get. It may seem a little awkward at first, if you have never used kettlebells before, but will be able to perfect your form, once you use kettlebells regularly. A lot of the exercises that involve kettlebells usually only require you to use one hand at once. This means you will need a little more coordination skills, as compares to using a barbell.

Workout Anywhere – I love kettlebells because you don't need that much space, you don't need to be indoors, and you certainly don't need a gym membership. You actually don't even need to buy your kettlebells at a store, you can make your own. (See "How To Choose Your Kettlebells" section later on in this book.)

Shoulder Pain – In the past I have had some issues with shoulder pain. It seemed every time I performed the bench press, my right shoulder started to hurt. This led to an imbalance in my chest. But once I started to perform kettlebells workouts I noticed that my shoulder pain went away. Kettlebells will help build up certain muscles in your shoulders, and this will help decrease your potential to injury. Kettlebells also increase the flexibly of joints in the shoulder that also prevent injury.

Chapter 2: How Heavy Should You Lift?

One of the most essential questions to ask when training with kettlebells, especially if you're just starting out, is how heavy should you lift? As mentioned earlier, excellent form is crucial for safe and effective kettlebell training and given that it involves unique dynamic movements that incorporate high intensity interval work periods, being able to use the right amount of weight is crucial.

As a beginner, you'll need to pay close attention to choosing the right weight to start off your kettlebell training program. But choosing the best kettlebell weight can be very challenging, especially if you've never done any sort of weight training before. It can seem that even the lightest kettlebell weight is too heavy.

On the other hand, maybe you've been lifting weights for quite a while now albeit with other traditional pieces of equipment like barbells, dumbbells, and suspension trainers. It's possible then that the weights I'll recommend may be "nothing but a peanut" to you. At this point, I'll need to ask you to momentarily suspend your current beliefs about weight or resistance training and instead, look at kettlebells from a fresh and different perspective. If you don't, you'll have a hard time appreciating what kettlebell training is and consequently, have a much harder time getting that shredded body you've been dreaming of.

It's very important that as you learn how to train with kettlebells that you practice what practically all trainers in the world ask of their trainees: have an open mind, pay attention, and learn. And while I believe you'll learn so much from this book to start training with kettlebells after, I still highly encourage you to perform at least one training session under the supervision of a seasoned kettlebell trainer to minimize injury risks using excellent form and maximizing the fat-burning and muscle-building effects of the exercises.

Keep in mind that kettlebell training isn't the same as the usual isolation training with weights. Many of the kettlebell training exercises are compound in nature, i.e., involves many muscle groups. Also, many of these exercises are full-body and require "throwing" the kettlebells around. It's highly unlikely you've done this type of training so it's important to start with an open mind and resist the temptation to believe that it's nothing new under the sun.

Training for at least a session or two with a professional kettlebell trainer will help you master the basic but more complex movements. And no amount of video or book training will ever match the level of detailed feedback and attention that a session or two with a kettlebell professional can give. And such feedback can help you maximize the body-shredding benefits and minimize injury risks during kettlebell training.

When you perform the kettlebell exercises using excellent form, you'll be able to improve your ability to control your body, significantly reduce your workout time, and achieve your goals, which include getting shredded of course! More than just getting shredded, you'll be able to do so sans the boredom! What a win-win proposition, eh?

From several core movements, kettlebell exercises have evolved into a plethora of new and exciting techniques and movements. And just like the slogan of one of the world's most popular junk foods go, once you start, you can't stop. Or at least you won't want to.

So now we go back to the question – how heavy should you lift?

For Men

For men, a good weight to start with for most exercises is 16 kilos or 35 pounds. If you're a guy, you may be thinking, "35 pounds is peanuts compared to my 100 pound bench press!" Hold on for a minute there, Sparky! While 35 pounds may be a light dumbbell or barbell weight, it's not necessarily a light kettlebell weight! Remember, kettlebells have a unique shape and handle!

If you really think about it, 35 pounds may not mean much to perform deadlifts, squats, or even barbell curls with! But since you won't be doing those particular exercises, at least not with a barbell, 35 pounds may actually mean more resistance than that which is available with barbells. This is because of the unique manner in which exercises are done using kettlebells.

Chances are, you'll be able to activate many muscles that you aren't able to with conventional weight or resistance training programs and equipment. You'll be able to wake up many of your "sleeping" muscles and believe me, many core muscles (upper legs, abs, and lower back) will feel as if they're being burned alive on your first session or two. This is because kettlebell training is normally paired with high intensity interval working sets, i.e., brief but very intense working stretches with very little – if any – rest in between sets.

Considering the above, you'll need to use a relatively low weight in proportion to your kettlebell training experience at the start, which in this case is more or less 35 pounds as a guy. If you find it to heavy, use a lighter kettlebell and if you feel it's too light, then adjust accordingly.

But don't take a 35-pound or 16-kilogram kettlebell for granted! Many men who are rookies to kettlebell training are at high risk for compromising proper form while performing kettlebell movements by either muscling or powering through movements. Why? It's because they use kettlebells that are beyond their abilities to lift using proper form. Ego? Perhaps.

On average, a 35-pound kettlebell should be enough for any male beginner to perform exercises with proper form. And as I've mentioned earlier, you can adjust accordingly by using a more appropriately weighted kettlebell.

For Women

If you're a woman, a very good weight to start with is an 18-pound or 8-kilogram kettlebell. As with the 35-pound kettlebell for men, this weight is an in-the-middle category that's good to start kettlebell training with.

When you first pick up the 18-pound kettlebell and try to do a single-arm upright row instinctively (i.e., no regard for proper lifting form), it's very tempting to think "Wow, that was easy. Wonder why the author ever suggested I start with this weight?" But as I mentioned earlier for men, a relatively "lighter" weight can actually feel much, much heavier when training with kettlebells because of its unique shape and handle. And such uniqueness can transform a dumbbell bicep curl, which is an isolation exercise, into a relatively compound one when done with kettlebells.

When you perform kettlebell exercises using proper form, you'll be able to train your body for much better body control, minimize the amount of time you'll need to work out per session to get shredded, and achieve your goals – both functional and aesthetic (i.e., a shredded body). With kettlebell training exercises, majority of your lifts will involve not just a leg or an arm but also your core, and your entire lower or upper body.

A Caution for both Men and Women

Many people believe that choosing the wrong working weight simply means working with a weight that's too heavy. You can also choose the wrong weight by lifting too light. Why is lifting too light also wrong?

Remember our emphasis on proper or excellent form? Well, lifting a very light weight puts you at high possibility of purely using your muscles or powering through ballistic movements instead of using proper form, which can be more challenging but stimulating to your muscles. When that happens, chances are you'll just throw weights around – with no regard for proper form – as if they were made of paper. And the more you stick to improper form, the less you'll be able to make significant progress in terms of weight load, strength, muscles, and shredding body fat. Hence, don't fall for the temptation that light is right. No... Right is right!

The Pood

No – it's not a tablet from an electronics manufacturer whose name is derived from a fruit that symbolizes temptation. When you're asked "What pood is the kettlebell you're using?" they're simply asking you how heavy is the kettlebell you're working with. In other words, a "pood" is a Russian unit of weight measurement. Just when you think there's only the American and British systems of measurement, here comes the Russians sowing even more confusion!

Anyhow, a pood is equivalent to about 16 kilos or 36 pounds. When you're into Crossfit and start to get into kettlebell training, you'll hear about this unit of measure more often.

Choosing the Best Kettlebell

More than just choosing the right kettlebell weight, you must be able to choose a quality kettlebell. Quality can impact your ability to train with kettlebells well so choose wisely. The following are good guidelines for choosing a high-quality kettlebell:

− Choose a kettlebell with a coating that's chip-resistant and smooth so that your hands won't be easily irritated, especially when you do stamina-building exercises for extended periods of time. A high quality kettlebell is one that has curved and smooth handles, which can be comfortably gripped at any point of the handle and not just on the top area.

– A high-quality kettlebell also has enough clearance or space in between the handle and the kettlebell itself to allow for maximum bone-stacking when performing press and snatch lifts. The obtuse shape of its handle must also make it easy to grip the sides of the kettlebell handle – also called horns – for specific exercises. And the handle's coating must be the same as that of the kettlebell's – smooth to minimize the risk of blisters, scratches, or wounds to your hands.

– High quality kettlebells are rust-free and are backed up by a lifetime warranty for such.

– Another characteristic of a high-quality kettlebell are high-contrast letterings that allow you to easily identify the particular kettlebell you're about to use.

– Lastly, a high quality kettlebell is one that you can comfortably grip. Factors that can affect your ability to grip your kettlebell include the width and diameter of the grips, the clearance between the top of the ball and the bottom of the handle, and the diameter of the kettle bell.

Now that we've got you all prepped up for kettlebell training, let's proceed to the workouts or exercises themselves. We've split these exercises into 3 chapters – one each for upper body, lower body, and combo or total body exercises. The key to achieving your ripped body is to train 3 times a week for 20 to 30 minutes straight, with very minimal rest in between sets and by minimal, I mean no more than 30 seconds per set. Aim to perform at least 3 sets per exercise and of course, use excellent form at all times.

Chapter 3: The Kettlebell And Crossfit Training

Because of the versatility of kettlebells to be included in the training regimen of any athlete, it is constantly used in the workout regimen of CrossFit practitioners. The practitioners who use this tool in their CrossFit programs are usually focused in improving strength and power.

If you are not familiar with CrossFit, it is a popular strength and conditioning program used in gyms all around the world. The program aims to improve your overall fitness through a series of high-intensity workouts. The three main types of workouts that you will do in CrossFit are aerobics, gymnastics and Olympic weight lifting exercises. The exercises that you do will vary each day. Some CrossFit gyms also design programs for practitioners with specific physical needs like sports training, martial arts training or professional fitness.

A typical CrossFit workout session will include a series of warm up exercises followed by skill development workout. Then, the Workout of the Day or the WoD will follow. Each individual gym has their own prescribed workout of the day but there are also some who follow the workout of the day suggested by the CrossFit website. The session usually ends with stretching exercises to cool down them muscles. There are some gyms who concentrate their WoDs on improving the strength like using Olympic weight lifting.

After the session, your performance in executing the workout of the day will be scored and ranked compared to other people that you worked out with. Other people also time their workouts. This practice makes the gym atmosphere even more competitive.

Using Kettlebells

For fitness buffs who have limited workout equipment at home, using the prescribed workout of the day will not be successful in yielding results because of the necessary tools to do certain tasks. This is where the kettlebell will come in handy. Instead of following the WoD in the CrossFit website or the local gym, you could start practicing CrossFit in your own home just by using kettlebells. You could do this by using the kettlebell workouts of the day found in this book.

This method is cheaper than joining a gym. It is also a lot more feasible than following the prescribed workout of the day in the CrossFit website. It is also a good option for beginners who are not yet confident about their ability to complete one CrossFit session.

Using the 30-day cycle

In the next chapter, you will see a 30-day routine using only kettlebells. A month long practice of these suggested workouts will help build enough muscles and stamina to prepare you for even more CrossFit trainings.

It is also better if you try to work out with a friend or a family member. Aside from the high-intensity workouts, CrossFit's success is greatly due to the community behind it. Make sure that you become a member of local CrossFit communities in your area. You could find some of them in local sports clubs and gyms. The community not only increases your sense of competition but can also be a good source of information and tips to become better.

Chapter 4: Big Muscles And Kettlebells

What are Big Muscles?

In general, muscles are divided into big and small muscles where big muscles consist of glutes, quadriceps, back, chest, and hamstrings. On the other side, small muscles mainly consist of shoulders, triceps, biceps, and calves. For the training purpose, it is important to first analyze how various muscle combinations can function well together during the workout and then opt for the muscles that are worked the hardest. However, it is suggested to choose big muscles to achieve higher intensities during the workout. The primary reason for it is that largest muscle groups allow the body to activate without body already being exhausted due to smaller muscle work. This will also enable an individual to lift more weight and will be able to control the body. As a result, it will increase the ability to coordinate movement and reduce chances of injury. Whereas, small muscles are used to stabilize for bigger muscles during the workout and are not able to train at high intensities. Due to this, the development of small muscles is limited.

Moreover, there are several ways to achieve maximum benefit, which include separating training of the larger and smaller muscle groups on different days. This will help to ensure that each muscle is trained at its maximal potential. In case, this is not a viable option then an individual can divide training into a course of 4 weeks where allot one week for small muscles training and three weeks of big muscles training. The primary reason for utilizing these muscles is that it helps to burn fat and builds strength. As muscles are used during the workout which helps build muscle mass, and muscle tissue, which in return burns more calories.

However, to burn fat, it is imperative to include both strength training and cardio exercises as it utilizes big muscles and helps to increase performance. For example, having strong glutes for running helps to go faster for longer time period, which burns more calories and doing exercises to strengthen the core can help you maintain form for biking, which can also help you burn more calories.

How Kettlebell Helps to Burn Fat

The kettlebell is an efficient equipment is today's time that can be used to work for the big muscles group. The kettlebell swing is considered as the fastest technique that can help to burn fat from the body without losing muscle mass and integrate a very athletic movement while increasing low-back stability simultaneously. This is because swing is powerful that involves big muscles and small muscles together which refines the muscles. Moreover, due to its dynamic athletic movement, it allows the body to produce the desired result depending on the body type. It also connects the upper body with the lower and produces functional strength instead of grouping body parts.

In addition to this, the kettlebell swing helps to burn fats in a short span of time and build muscle mass. It also helps to create high heart rates with relative lightweights. The swing further enhances the physique while simultaneously increasing the cardiovascular strength and endurance. Numerous studies indicated that twenty minutes of continuous kettlebell training could burn calories equal to running at a six-minute mile pace. However, the rate at which an individual can burn the fat is difficult is interpret, though if the training is of hard intensity and a controlled diet is followed, then it is anticipated to lose in the region of 1 to 2 pounds per week. Even though kettlebell usually produces faster results but the rate to burn fat varies due to the number of factors involved during the kettlebell training.

Chapter 5: Tips To Get An Edge In Training

Think of your body as a stool with three legs; nutrition, exercise and sleep. If you are falling short in any of these areas then you will be both compromising your health and your results in the other two areas. Research has shown that sleep deprived (less than 7 hours) test subjects lost less fat than the test subjects on an identical exercise and nutritional protocol. Another example is undertaking a gruelling workout regime only to fuel yourself with pizza after. This sabotages your hard work, as you are not giving your body the nutrients it requires to repair itself efficiently. Below are the cliff notes to ensure you have a solid stool.

Nutrition:

Liquids= water and lots of it (1litre when you wake up), or green tea.

Food= lean protein (fish, chicken and beef)

Vegetables (the more colour the better especially leafy greens)

Energy/fats (coconut oil for cooking, olive oil for dressing, nuts including almonds, brazil, cashews, walnut and peanut butter.)

Carbohydrates (fruit directly before and after exercise, porridge and sweet potato before and after hard trainings.)

Supplements (Protein powder, fish oil and vitamin D 5000 -10000IU/day.)

Fasting once a month for 2-3days, I'm a big fan of fasting and recommend it be undertaken regularly to help reset your system.

Exercise: Concentrate on compound moves such as squat presses, pull-ups, Turkish getups renegade rows, Burpees, etc. The more muscle groups involved in a move, the better for calorie burn and the functionality of the move. Maintain 20rep sets for conditioning and 5rep sets for strength. HIIT training can also turbo charge your fat loss and conditioning. Training first thing in the morning on an empty stomach has resulted in rapid fat loss for me personally. It is hard and you can feel quite weak during the workout, which is not ideal, but if you want an edge and quick results then you can consider this. Surprise your body, as it has a remarkable ability to adapt. If you feel you are cruising through the workout then try a boxing or Crossfit class. It will surprise your body into adapting again and jump start your results. No workout should ever be over 45mins (30mins is ideal) - hard and fast/efficient is always best!

SleepRules:

7 hours a night minimum.

Cut out blue light (given off by laptops, tablets and smart phone screens) at least two hours prior to bed (as it messes with your melatonin.)

Alternatively download F.lux (free app which cuts down blue light given off by your screen the later it gets.)

Ensure a cool dark room (use thick light blocking curtains) to ensure an optimal sleeping environment.

Don't have caffeine after 12pm (you'll be surprised how long caffeine remains in your system.)

Don't use your bedroom for anything other than sleep (and sex), so get rid of the TV and the laptop in bed, as when you get into bed your body should only associate it with sleeping.

Lastly our bodies love routine; you should ensure that your bedtime and waking time to do not change significantly, so that your body gets used to the schedule.

Try yoga, as maintaining flexibility is an important consideration as we age. A high proportion of the population suffers from poor hip and hamstrings flexibility due to our modern requirement to sit in a car on the way to the office, to sit in a chair all day followed by sitting in the car on the way home, then sitting and watching TV and, well, you get the idea! Opening up tight hips through regular yoga practice is an amazing feeling and one of the main reasons I recommend you find time for yoga at least once a week. Protecting posture is also an important consideration, as posture directly effects people's impression of you and helps you show off your hard work in the gym and present yourself with confidence

Train in thin-soled shoes with no heel, preferably shoes were you can feel the ground, thus giving the muscles in your feet the opportunity to develop. Modern running shoes have completely disengaged the foot from the ground and can cause the poor form of heel striking when running. You will be surprised at the role strong feet can play in lifts such as squats, swings and box jumps. It can also help relieve low back pain training in flat shoes as it maintains the body's alignment and prevents the back arching to compensate.

Lastly you are the average of the five people you spend the most time with. Really think about this - are the people around you supporting you or quietly trying to sabotage your efforts? For instance friends that always suggest getting desert, or mock you for getting the salad. You know who these people are and the real question is; are you going to accept the effect these people have on your life or find people that point you in the right direction. A good training partner is worth their weight in gold, holding you accountable to sessions, reps and sets.

Kettlebell Cardio

Kettlebell cardio involves picking one of three exercise choices; the kettlebell swing, kettlebell squat and press or kettlebell snatchs illustrated below. Weight is reduced, basically if you normally use a 24kg kettlebell you would drop to 20kg. Repetitions are your body weight (in kilograms) in as many sets as required. I'm 90kgs and it took me 3 sets of 30 reps to achieve the 90 total reps. The aim is to work up to your full body weight and to eventually complete a single set.

Hand Care

A side effect of high rep kettlebell training can be calluses and if you are not careful blisters. Below are a few tips to help keep your hands in good shape.

File down calluses to keep them smooth. This is best done with a nail file immediately after showering or having a bath when your skin is softest.

Avoid standard moisturisers as they can soften your hands more than necessary making your hands more susceptible to blisters. I've found coconut oil to be the best compromise with the bonus of it being naturally antibacterial.

If you do tear or blister your hands take a week off and apply coconut oil to your hands twice daily. If a week off isn't an option concentrate on body weight exercises for the week i.e. squats, burpees, pushups and lunges.

Try to gloves if possible as it reduces your ability to grip the kettlebell and makes the exercises harder. However if you are a beautician or hand model then very thin glove liners should be or go to as proper lifting gloves are far too thick. If you are on a budget just grab a thin sock and it cut into two tubes then snip a thumb hole into each.

Snatchs

The whole movement should be one fluid, continuous action with no jerkiness. At no point should the kettlebell be banging into forearm, as you should be punching through the kettlebell at the top of the movement. The kettlebell should be reaching the back of your forearm at exactly the same time as when your elbow locks. The movement should be created entirely by your hip drive, the be no pressing of the kettlebell at all. The kettlebell needs to come off your hand as soon as you drop it to avoid tearing up your hand.

Develops impressive explosiveness and feels great performing the move.

Will build a solid back, hip, and fingers; while developing great cardio-respiratory endurance.

Can represent an entire cardio workout if done for high repetitions (The U.S Special Forces tests total snatchs with a 24kg kettlebell in 10mins with 200 being the general aim!)

A vital part of the snatch is ensuring the kettlebell is not hitting the back of your forearm with force. The aim is to close the distance between your forearm and the kettlebell as quickly as possible. To visualise this it is the idea you must 'punch' up through the kettlebells arc rather than stop and let it fall over the top of the movement and crash into your forearm.

You should aim to sharply exhale at the top of the movement before breathing into your stomach via your nose on the way down.

Watch the snatch movement on YouTube as the below illustration does not do the movement justice.

Start with your feet a little wider than shoulder width apart with the kettlebell between your feet.

Bend your knees and push your hips back, bending at the waist while keeping your back straight.

Grip the kettle bell with an overhand grip.

Keeping your neck and head straight, swing the kettlebell back between your legs.

Once the kettlebell is behind you, immediately reverse the direction and drive forward with your hips and knees, forcing the kettlebell upward and snatch it overhead in one uninterrupted motion to a straight arm lockout.

Catch the Kettlebell softly without banging your forearm, and ensuring your arm at lockout is level with your head or behind your head.

Use your body's downward momentum to receive the weight as it comes back down in a loose uninterrupted motion without touching the chest or shoulder.

Alternating Lunges

Strengthens glutes and hip flexors, helping to build power and explosiveness.

Do it without kettlebells until you have a good rhythm and foundation for the move.

You can add a plyometric aspect by using lighter weights and jumping between lunges.

Gripping a kettlebell in each hand, stand with your feet shoulder-width apart.

Keep your back straight and shoulders back.

Lunge forward with your right leg. Your right foot should be in a position, that when you bend your right knee, your upper and lower leg forms a 90-degree angle.

Slowly bend both your knees, to lower your hips until your left (rear) knee is just above the floor.

Return to the start position by slowly straightening your legs and raising your body back to a standing position.

Complete all the repetitions for one set full set, then switch legs, or you can alternate between legs for each rep.

Note: Do not let your knee travel past your toes in the down position, as this can cause instability and injury.

Burpees (Build up to doing this with two kettlebells)

Great finisher at the end of a workout

Good substitute for boring cardio, as you can achieve a lot in short bursts of Burpees.

Aim for 20 x reps and 3 x sets or timed intervals (3x3mins.)

Stand straight with your feet shoulder width apart and hands by your sides.

In one smooth motion, squat down and place your hands palms down on the floor in front of your feet.

Lean forward, so your weight is on your hands, at the same time jumping your legs out behind you until they are fully extended. Your body should form a straight line with your weight supported on your toes and the balls of your feet and your arms fully extended. Essentially in a push-up position.

Jump your feet out by spreading your legs, so that they are wider than hip width apart, then immediately jump them back together.

Complete one full push up.

Jump your feet forward to just behind your hands.

Use an explosive motion to push through your heels and return to the start position.

Repeat.

Chapter 6: Kettlebell Workouts For Beginners

In this chapter, to help you get started, I'm going to provide you with three beginner-friendly kettlebell workouts that anybody can do.

Upper body

Core

Lower body

Beginners should start off easy and slow. Before you even bring your kettlebell into the workout, perform the exercises without the added weight. Feel your body move through the motions, be mindful of instability or balance problems. Work on your form and ensure that you are using correct form before performing any of the exercises with your kettlebells. Remember it is vital to perfect your form to prevent injury and get the most out of your kettlebell workout.

Tip: It is always worthwhile considering booking a session or two with an instructor to help you perfect your form. A professional can observe your movement objectively from various angles and provide guidance to ensure that you are performing each movement in an exercise correctly.

Lunges and Squats: When performing lunges and squats, only perform the exercise as far as is comfortable. If you have trouble knee joints, keep your squats and lunges higher to avoid discomfort. As you get stronger, try to take them lower if you can. If you can't take them any lower, perform the exercises at a level that is comfortable for you.

When to increase weight or reps: Please refer to Chapter 8 for guidelines on when to increase your kettlebell weight or repetitions and sets.

THE RACKED POSITION

I will be referring to the racked position throughout the next three chapters on kettlebell workouts. It is important to understand this holding position and to perfect it. That way you will avoid injury and bruising.

Grip your kettlebell handle so that it rests diagonally across your palm. The handle should lead from the crook of your thumb on the one side to the base of your palm and wrist on the other side.

During the racked hold or position, your kettlebell is held against your chest at shoulder height with your elbow bent. The body of your kettlebell rests against your outer forearm.

POOR RACK FORM

When the racked hold is not done correctly, you risk injury by placing unnecessary strain on your wrist, forearm, elbow, and shoulder. There are two reasons for incorrect rack form.

Your kettlebell handle is positioned directly across the center of your palm instead of diagonally.

You are holding your kettlebell to the side, closer to your shoulder, and not close enough to your chest.

FLOPPING

When using the racked position during exercises, it is important to control your grip of the handle as it rotates through your palm. When you are lowering your kettlebell from a racked position, the handle will naturally rotate in your palm to bring the kettlebell forward. When you are bringing your kettlebell up into the racked position the handle will naturally rotate in your palm to flip the kettlebell towards the back of your hand. It will come to rest against your outer forearm.

If you do not have grip control, you could end up flopping your kettlebell against your outer forearm when bringing it into the racked hold. This is a painful experience and often leaves bruises. The good news is that as your grip strength and control of your kettlebell increases, you will be able to stop the flop.

BEGINNER UPPER BODY KETTLEBELL WORKOUT

Pull Up	8 - 10	3 - 5
Press	8 - 10 per side	3 - 5
Clean	8 - 10 per side	3 - 5
Regular Row	8 - 10 per side	3 - 5
Pull Over	8 - 10	3 - 5

Rest period between sets: 30 seconds to two minutes, decrease the rest time as you progress, and get fitter.

PULL UP

Muscles targeted: shoulders, upper back, glutes, hamstrings, quads

Gripping your kettlebell handle firmly with both hands, stand with it hanging down in front of your body. Your kettlebell should be hanging at about thigh height.

Bring your kettlebell up to your chest by bending your elbows out sideways. Once your kettlebell is at chest height, your arms should be parallel to the ground.

Extend your arms downward and lower your kettlebell back to thigh height.

Variation: Squat Pull Up

Add some leg drive to your pull up by performing a squat while your kettlebell is hanging at thigh height. As you push up out of the squat, raise your kettlebell into the pull up. As you lower your kettlebell back to thigh height, squat down again and repeat.

PRESS

Muscles targeted: shoulders, triceps, core

Stand with your feet shoulder-width apart and start with your kettlebell held in the racked position.

Extend your arm upwards, raising your kettlebell overhead. Be sure to hold your kettlebell directly over your shoulder so that your shoulder, elbow, and wrist are in line with each other.

Lower your kettlebell back to the racked position.

Variation: Push Press

To add a bit of oomph to your press, perform a half squat while holding your kettlebell in the racked position. As you push up from the half squat to a standing position, use the momentum to extend your arm into the press.

CLEAN

Muscles targeted: Shoulders, back, core, quads, glutes, hamstrings

Stand with your feet shoulder-width apart, holding your kettlebell in the racked position. This is the same position that you will finish your repetition in.

Extend your elbow and swing your kettlebell in a downward arc. As it is swinging downward, bend your knees and hinge your torso forward from your hips, allowing your kettlebell to swing between your legs.

As your kettlebell swings forward again, straighten your legs and torso back into a standing position. While straightening up, thrust your hips forward, the power from your hip thrust will add momentum to your kettlebell's upward swing.

As your kettlebell swings upwards, bend your elbow and bring it back into the racked position.

REGULAR ROW

Muscles targeted: shoulders, biceps, back, core, glutes, quads, hamstrings

Stand in a relaxed, neutral position; feet shoulder-width apart, with your kettlebell between your feet.

Bend your knees and hinge forward from your hips.

Grip your kettlebell with one hand.

Pull your kettlebell towards your ribs by bending your elbow and pulling back toward the ceiling.

Keep your elbow tucked in next to your body to prevent your arm from moving out to the side.

Lower your kettlebell by extending your arm again but to not set your kettlebell down on the floor. Hold it about an inch off the ground.

While performing the row exercise; maintain a straight back and keep your shoulders level. Do not allow the shoulder of the arm you are holding your kettlebell in to drop.

Variation: Double Kettlebell Row

If you have two kettlebells of the same weight, you can perform the row using both kettlebells to increase the difficulty of this exercise.

PULL OVER

Muscles targeted: shoulders, triceps, back, core

Start by lying on your back on the floor with your kettlebell on the floor above your head.

Reach your arms above your head to grip your kettlebell on either side of the handle.

Keeping your arms straight, lift your kettlebell up and over your head until your arms are straight. Your wrists, elbows, and shoulders should be in line with each other.

Lower your kettlebell back to the ground above your head but don't set it down; keep it about an inch off the floor.

Variation: Pull Over Hip Raise

As you advance, you can make your pull over do double duty. When you have raised your kettlebell overhead, hold the position. While holding this position, keep both legs together and raise them off the ground so that your legs are pointing up toward the ceiling. Contract your core muscles to raise your legs and hips off the floor for a count of one before lowering your hips and straightening your legs back onto the floor.

BEGINNER CORE WORKOUT

Exercise	Reps	Sets
Windmill	4 - 5 per side	3 - 5
Lunge with rotation	8 - 10	3 - 5
Sit up	8 - 10	3 - 5
Farmer's carry	45 - 60 seconds per side	3 - 5
Figure eight	8 - 10 in each direction (left and right)	3 - 5

Rest period between sets: 30 seconds to two minutes, decrease the rest time as you progress, and get fitter.

WINDMILL

Muscles targeted: shoulders, core, glutes, hamstrings

Stand with your feet shoulder-width apart, your weight leaned into your right hip and your left leg slightly extended to the side.

Hold your kettlebell in the rack position in your right hand.

Extend your right arm to raise your kettlebell overhead. Be sure to hold your kettlebell directly over your shoulder so that your shoulder, elbow, and wrist are in line with each other.

Your left arm should be extended by your side.

Rotate your torso slightly to bring your left shoulder forward.

Bend sideways to the left, pushing your weight into your right hip.

Only bend sideways as far as is comfortable. If you cannot touch the ground, that's okay.

Maintain a straight right arm holding your kettlebell overhead. Don't bend your elbow or allow your arm to lean.

Straighten up to the original starting position.

LUNGE WITH ROTATION

Muscles targeted: shoulders, core, quads, hamstrings, glutes

Stand with your feet shoulder-width apart.

Grip your kettlebell with both hands at either side of the handle and hold it to your chest.

Step into a lunge position by either stepping back into a reverse lunge or forward into a regular lunge.

As you perform the lunge, rotate your torso to the side so that you are looking to the side without turning your head.

Return to a standing position, rotating your torso back to the front as you do so.

Tip: If rotating your torso while performing the lunge is too challenging, perform the lunge and hold while you rotate your torso. Rotate your torso back to the front before returning to the starting position.

SIT UP

Muscles targeted: core, back, shoulders

Sit on the floor. Your legs should either be straight in front of you or bent at the knee, similar to the position for regular sit-ups.

Grip your kettlebell on either side of the handle and bring it to your chest.

Lie back on the floor, holding your kettlebell to your chest.

Perform a regular sit up while holding your kettlebell lightly against your chest. Don't push it out forward or let it sink into your lap.

Lower yourself back onto the floor.

Be sure to engage your core muscles to perform the sit up and not your lower back to prevent injury.

FARMER'S CARRY

Muscles targeted: core, shoulders, obliques, forearms

Stand with your feet shoulder-width apart and your kettlebell gripped firmly in one hand at your side.

Walk forward, engaging your core muscles to keep your torso straight. Keeping your shoulders level. Do not lean to the side, backward, or forward.

Keep your kettlebell as still as possible throughout. You may need to hold it slightly away from your body to prevent it from bumping.

Instead of multiple repetitions, each set will consist of walking with your kettlebell for 45-60 seconds.

FIGURE-EIGHT

Muscles targeted: core, shoulders, glutes, quads, hamstrings

Stand with your feet slightly wider than shoulder-width apart, knees slightly bent and torso hinged forward from the hips.

Gripping your kettlebell in your left hand, swing it around your left side from front to back.

As you swing the kettlebell around your left side, reach your right hand between your legs to pass your kettlebell from your left hand to your right hand as it passes behind your left leg.

With your right hand, bring your kettlebell forward between your legs and swing it around your right side from front to back.

Reach your left hand between your legs to pass it back from your right hand to your left hand as it swings around the back of your right leg.

The kettlebell is being swung in a figure-eight motion around and between your legs.

Be sure to maintain a straight back throughout.

BEGINNER LOWER BODY WORKOUT

Two-handed Kettlebell Swing	8 - 10	3 - 5
Two-handed dead lift	8 - 10	3 - 5
Goblet squat	8 - 10	3 - 5
Two-handed lunge	8 - 10	3 - 5
Side Lunge	8 - 10 per side	3 - 5
Bob and weave	8 - 10 to each side	3 - 5

Rest period between sets: 30 seconds to two minutes, decrease the rest time as you progress, and get fitter.

TWO-HANDED KETTLEBELL SWING

Muscles targeted: quads, glutes, hamstrings, shoulders, core, back

Stand with your feet shoulder-width apart, knees slightly bent, and torso hinged forward from the hips. Keep your back straight while your torso is hinged forward.

Grip the top of your kettlebell handle with both hands.

Lift your kettlebell off the ground and allow it to swing back between your legs.

Straighten up to a standing position, thrusting your hips forward. The hip thrust will offer momentum to your kettlebell swing.

Swing your kettlebell out in front of you in an arch until it reaches chest height while keeping your arms straight.

As your kettlebell swings downward again, bend your knees and hinge your torso forward from the hips and allow the kettlebell to swing between your legs.

TWO-HANDED DEADLIFT

Muscles targeted: glutes, hamstrings, quads, back, core

Stand in a relaxed, neutral position; feet shoulder-width apart, with your kettlebell between your feet.

Bend your knees and hinge your torso forward from the hips. Keep your back straight.

Grip your kettlebell firmly by the handle with both hands.

Straighten up to a standing position, lifting your kettlebell with you. Your kettlebell should be hanging in front of your body at thigh level.

Bend your knees and hinge your torso forward from the hips to place your kettlebell back on the ground between your feet.

GOBLET SQUAT

Muscles targeted: Hamstrings, glutes, quads, core

Stand with your feet shoulder-width apart. Grip your kettlebell on either side of the handle, holding it upside down against your chest.

Bend your knees and hinge your torso forward from the hips to perform a squat.

Return to a standing position.

Variation: Goblet Squat Press

To spice up your goblet squat, add a press to your exercise. When you push off out of the squat position to a standing position, raise your kettlebell overhead to perform a press. Lower your kettlebell to chest height again before performing the next squat.

TWO-HANDED LUNGE

Muscles targeted: shoulders, core, hamstrings, glutes, quads

Stand with your feet shoulder-width apart. Grip your kettlebell on either side of the handle and hold against your chest.

Step into a lunge position by either stepping back into a reverse lunge or forward into a regular lunge.

Return to the standing position.

Variation: Double Kettlebell Lunge

If you have two kettlebells of the same weight, you can hold both kettlebells at your sides while performing the lunge for added resistance and difficulty.

SIDE LUNGE

Muscles targeted: glutes, hamstrings, quads, shoulders, back, core

Stand with your feet shoulder-width apart. Grip your kettlebell on either side of the handle and hold against your chest.

Step to your right, bending your right knee and lowering yourself into a side lunge with your left leg extended out to the side. Push your hips backward and hinge your torso slightly forward during the lunge.

Keep your kettlebell high against your chest to prevent unnecessary pressure on your lower back.

Return to the standing position.

Variation: Side Lunge Press

Take your side lunge up a notch. Hold the side lunge position while you raise your kettlebell overhead to perform a press. Lower your kettlebell to chest height again before returning to a standing position.

BOB AND WEAVE

Muscles targeted: hamstrings, glutes, quads, core, back

Stand feet shoulder-width apart, gripping your kettlebell on either side of the handle and holding it to your chest.

Using your right leg, take a wide step to the right.

As you step, hinge your torso forward from the hips and 'duck' in a squat-type position before straightening up and bringing your left leg to the right to resume a standing position.

When performing the bob and weave, imagine that there is a low beam next to you. You need to get to the other side of the beam by stepping to the side and ducking under the beam, before straightening up on the other side of the beam.

Chapter 7: Advanced Exercises

Advanced routines are for people who are looking for more challenging kettlebell exercises. Keep your safety in mind while doing the exercise.

Alternating renegade row

Targets: middle back

Place two kettlebells on the floor with your feet apart. Place your toes and hands on the ground in a plank position. Keep your body straight and extended. Use the kettlebells as a support for your upper body. Push one kettlebell to the floor and row the other kettlebell. Retract your shoulder blade and flex your elbows pulling it to your side. Lower the kettlebell to the floor and switch the kettlebell to the other hand. Repeat several times.

Double Kettlebell Alternating Hang Clean

Targets: hamstrings, biceps, forearms

Stand with your feet apart. Place two kettlebells in front of you. Get into the starting position by pushing your back and keeping your head straight. Clean one kettlebell to your shoulders while holding on to the other. Quickly lower the top kettlebell while pulling the bottom kettlebell up. Do as much repetition in a minute as possible.

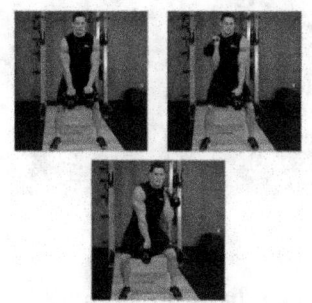

Plyo kettlebell pushup

Targets: chest, shoulders

Place the kettlebell on the floor. Drop into a plank position with your toes on the ground. Keep one arm on the floor while the other is holding on to the kettlebell. Keep your elbows extended. Begin to lower your body as low as you can while keeping your back straight. Quickly reverse the direction of your movement while pushing the other kettlebell. Switch your hands as you progress. Continue the movement and repeat it back and forth.

Open palm kettlebell clean

Targets: Hamstrings, glutes, lower back

Place the kettlebell on the floor. Hold it by the handle and pull it up by extending your arm and passing it through your legs and hips. Raise the kettlebell to your shoulders. Release the kettlebell in front of you and catch the handle with both of your hands. Lower the kettlebell and repeat the movement.

One arm kettlebell split snatch

Targets: shoulders, hamstrings, quadriceps

Hold one kettlebell in one hand and squat. Quickly reverse the motion while extending the hips and knees. Raise the kettlebell over your head. After extending your body, descend in a lunge position while pushing the kettlebell over your head. Keep one leg forward and one leg back. Make sure to move your hips and lock the kettlebell over your head in a fluid motion. Stand up with the kettlebell over your head. Bring your feet together then lower the kettlebell.

Kettlebell pistol squat

Targets: Quadriceps, calves

Hold the kettlebell by the horns using two hands. Keep one leg off the floor and squat with the other leg. Squat low and flex the knee while sitting back. Place the kettlebell in front of you. Pause for a few seconds then reverse the movement while keeping your head and chest straight. Lower your body and repeat the motion.

Bent press

Targets: abdominals, hamstrings, lower back, shoulders

Clean the kettlebell by passing it through your legs and hips. Raise it towards your shoulders and rotate your wrists as you move. Lean to the opposite side of the kettlebell. Continue until you are able to touch the ground with your free hand. Remember to keep your eyes on the kettlebell. Press the weight vertically using your elbows and keep your arm perpendicular to the ground. Stand up with the kettlebell above your head. Place the kettlebell to your shoulder and repeat the movement few more times.

Chapter 8: Stretching Out And Warming Up

I don't mean to be one of these guys, but what you've traditionally heard about stretching is wrong.

You may think that every workout starts with holding a butterfly, touching your toes and doing a leg extension, like in gym class as a kid, but recent evidence is suggesting that this isn't the most effective way to prepare your body for exercise. Instead, you want to create a situation where you perform light movements to warm up your joints and muscles and begin to create some heat in your body to the point of breaking into a gentle sweat. Static stretching does not accomplish this, but dynamic, full body movements and light intensity work does.

A different approach

Instead of this traditional, stretch-before-you-train model, I will make 3 simple suggestions of how to structure your mobility routine. Indeed, what we are going for is an entire framework of mobility and stability. If you want to really get good information on this, consider the books Becoming a Supple Leopard or The Roll Model

1. dynamic movements with single stretch

2. morning or nighttime stretching

3. single leg and single arm stability drills

Dynamic movements

Dynamic movements are ways to warm up muscles and joints before a rigorous workout. Instead of static stretching, a dynamic warm up incorporates full-body movements. I'll usually start from the top of my head and work my way down.

Neck rotations

Arm circles

Arm swings

Cross body arm swings

Band pass-through

Trunk rotation

Hip circles

Leg swings

Side to side leg swings

Ankle circles

Air squats

I'll usually follow this up with something like:

4 minutes of jump rope

or

800 meter run

or

4 minutes of rowing

Mobility and stretching

Stretching is something you want to get in the habit of doing hours in advance or after your work out. Stretching before a workout has been shown to not significantly increase performance, and recent research has even suggested that stretching immediately before a workout can even have a negative overall impact.

My preferred method of stretching is based in yin yoga. Yin is a style of yoga I have been practicing for almost 8 years where you hold static poses for 2-5 minutes and breathe with deep, rhythmic breath patterns. As far as I have experienced, it is one of the best ways to open up the body, repair sensitive muscles, relieve stress (which is very important during a heavy block of training) and creative mobility.

Search online for yin yoga routines, and if you want an amazing paid web service to guide your stretching routine I couldn't recommend www.romwod.com enough. You can also add stretch bands and straps to increase the effectiveness of the stretching routine.

Another method for creating mobility is releasing sore and tense muscles with the use of foam rollers, massage sticks and balls. This is an advanced method and I recommend buying and studying a book like Becoming a Supple Leopard or The Roll Model to give yourself a clear picture of what this looks like.

For a night time foam rolling sessions I'll typically do something like:

2 minutes of rolling the bottom of each foot with a lacrosse ball

3 minutes attacking each leg with a foam roller

2 minutes focused on rolling my back and neck

2 minutes on each hip with a lacrosse or kinesio ball

This 9-10 minute routine will loosen up tight muscles, mobilize my spine and neck, move blood and help me recover from training.

Stability training

Stability refers to your ability to stay static and resist motion when necessary. The demands of an obstacle race mean that stability is of the upmost importance. There are tons of little muscles and connective tissues that lead to overall general stability and these can be trained like the bigger muscle groups. Below is a sample workout that can be used to build stability and single-leg mobility.

1. 4 x 10 single leg dead lift (using a dumbbell or kettlebell)

2. Single arm snatch to overhead squat (using a dumbbell or kettlebell)

3. 4 x 8 single leg TRX or band assisted pistols

4. 1 minute warrior 3 pose on each leg for 3 rounds

5. 1 minute side plank hold for 3 rounds

Another great way to build stability is with an agility ladder. Look up agility ladder workouts on YouTube and you can find some awesome examples of how to incorporate this into your training. It's a great warm up tool if nothing else!

By merging together all of these pieces, you will make your body more durable, free of nagging injuries and more full recovered.

Off days

Off days are as important as training days, and you can't expect to train every day without a break – this will lead to overtraining syndrome and overuse injuries. But, these off days can still function as a major part of your training if you use them correctly.

Off days are a time to focus in on the mobility drills we talked about above. Spend an hour doing yoga or 30 extra minutes stretching and rolling.

Otherwise, use this time to plan and prep your meals so you are eating with good quality all week. If you're feeling really torched, go for a long walk, enjoy nature and maybe think about building something with your hands. Take the time to plan your extra training sessions and make a schedule for training.

The bottom line is this — there are no off days, but that doesn't mean you have to throw down every day of the week. Just make you off days as productive as your training days.

Chapter 9: Optimized Soviet Kettlebell Routines

In this chapter, we'll present you with training regimens targeted toward 2 distinct training goals:

Fat Loss

Muscle Gain

We'll give you 3 workouts for each of these goals, allowing you to progress your training from beginner to advanced level.

The Tabata Protocol

Your Fat Loss workouts will incorporate an advanced cardio regimen that will ramp you fat burn into the stratosphere. It's called the Tabata Protocol

The Tabata Protocol all began with the Japanese Olympic Speed Skating Team. The Head Coach, Irisawa Koichi, created a High Intensity Interval Training Workout for his skaters. This consisted of 8 rounds.

Each round was 20 seconds of intense work using a cycling ergometer followed by 10 seconds of rest. Koichi had one of his training coaches, Azumi Tabata, analyze the effectiveness of this workout using scientific methods. This is where the Tabata Protocol (which HIIT training is based upon) came about. Tabata didn't actually invent the training method, but because of widespread interest in his findings the workout was named after him. Tabata's studies showed his subjects producing impressive results that make traditional (steady state) cardio seem ineffective by comparison.

To perform the Tabata Protocol with Kettlebells simply perform the movement for 20 seconds and then take a 10 seconds rest. Repeat for the stated number of sets.

The Fat Loss Workouts

Beginner Workout for Fat Loss

Warm-Up

Around-the-body pass : 30 s each direction with light kettlebell

Halo : 30 s each direction with light kettlebell

Kettlebell deadlift: 10 reps

Goblet squat : 10 reps

Workout

Two Handed Kettlebell Swing: Tabata protocol for 20 s with 10 s rest before alternating arms. Repeat for 4 sets with 1 min recovery between sets.

Single Press: Tabata protocol for 20 s with 10 s rest before alternating arms. Repeat for 4 sets with 1 min recovery between sets.

Warm-Down

Easy jog for 10 min

Stretch for 5 min: 30 s each side for each stretch (behind-the-back shoulder stretch; shoulder stretch, triceps pulls, standing knee-to-chest stretch, standing quadriceps stretch

Intermediate Workout for Fat Loss

Warm-Up

Two-arm single-leg kettlebell deadlift : 8 reps on each side

Windmill : 10 reps on each side

Joint mobility exercises : Rotate all major joints (shoulders, hips, neck) 10-20 times.

Workout

Perform as many rounds as possible in 10 min:

Double swing : 15 reps with medium-weight kettlebells

Double clean : 15 reps with medium-weight kettlebells

Double front squat : 15 reps with medium-weight kettlebells

Russian twist : 40 twists with medium-weight kettlebell

Warm-Down

Easy jog for 10 min

Stretch for 5 min: 30 s each side for each stretch (behind-the-back shoulder stretch; shoulder stretch, triceps pulls, standing knee-to-chest stretch, pg. standing quadriceps stretch

Advanced Workout for Fat Loss

Warm-Up

Easy jog for 5 min

Dynamic mobility exercises: arm twirls forward and backward for 30s, dynamic clapping for 30 s, leg swings in each direction for 30 s

Workout

Goblet squat : 30 s each side

Spinal flexion : hold for 1 min

Calf stretch : 1 min per leg

Two Arm Kettlebell Row: Tabata protocol for 20 s with 10 s rest. Repeat for 4 sets.

Lunge Clean / Lunge Press: Tabata protocol for 20 s with 10 s rest. Repeat for 4 sets.

Static stretches: 30 s each side or 10 reps each exercise (standing quadriceps stretch; standing hamstrings stretch;

standing knee-to-chest stretch; calf stretch; spinal flexion)

The Muscle Gain Workouts

Beginner Workout for Muscle Gain

Easy jog for 5 min

Joint mobility exercises: Rotate all major joints (shoulders, hips, neck) 10-20 times or for 5 min.

Perform 10 reps of each of the following exercises on each side of the body without stopping. Repeat for 3 rounds with 1 min rest between each round. One round consists of the single swing, single clean, single press, snatch, and goblet squat.

Stretch for 7 min: Perform each stretch for 1 min (behind-the-back shoulder stretch; standing knee-to-chest stretch; standing hamstrings stretch; standing quadriceps stretch; spinal extension; child's pose; spinal flexion).

Intermediate Workout for Muscle Gain

Warm-Up

Easy jog for 5 min

Body-weight squat: 1 set for 30 s

Joint mobility exercises: 20 reps of each (hip circles, trunk twists, lateral bends, waist bends, shoulder rolls, neck tilts, neck rotations, ankle bounces).

Workout

Rack hold: Hold for 2 min with two light kettlebells, rest 1 min, hold 2 min with two moderate-weight kettlebells, rest 2 min, hold 1 min with two heavy kettlebells.

Overhead hold: Hold 1 min with two light kettlebells, rest 1 min, hold 1 min with two moderate-weight kettlebells.

Single Arm Press: Do 2 sets of 5 reps per hand, resting 1 min between sets.

Two Arm Kettlebell Rows: Do 3 sets of 10 reps, resting 1 min between sets.

Russian Twist: Do 3 sets of 15 reps, resting 1 min between each set.

Farmer's Carry: Hold two heavy kettlebells for as long as possible for 1 set.

Warm-Down

Easy jog for 5 min

Stretch for 7 min: Perform each stretch for 1 min (behind-the-back shoulder stretch; standing knee-to-chest stretch; standing hamstrings stretch; standing quadriceps stretch; spinal extension; child's pose; spinal flexion).

Advanced Workout for Muscle Gain

Warm-Up

Body-weight squat: 1 set of 30 reps

Skipping rope: 1 min

Dynamic mobility exercises: 15 reps of each arm twirls in both directions; chest hollow and expand; vertical chest opener; dynamic clapping; leg swings

Workout

Turkish Get-up: 5 reps each arm

Goblet Squat: 5 sets of 5 reps, resting 1 min between sets

One Arm Clean: 1 min, rest 1 min

Snatch: 1 min, rest 1 min

High Pull: 5 sets of 10 reps, resting 1 min between sets

Warm-Down

Easy jog for 10 min

Stretch for 7 min: Perform each stretch for 1 min (behind-the-back shoulder stretch; standing knee-to-chest stretch; standing hamstrings stretch; standing quadriceps stretch; spinal extension; child's pose; spinal flexion).

Chapter 10: Kettlebell Fat Loss Workout

The workout has been specifically designed for any individual whose primary goal is to lose maximum amount of fat from his/her body; the workout features low weight, high rep techniques to accomplish this task.

The tools of trade required for this workout will be:

For women – 8 kg pair of kettlebells,

For men – 16 kg pair of kettlebells

The weights would serve both a beginner as well as an intermediate.

A 5 kg medicine ball, if not available then you may use a bundle of water bottles or weight plates instead.

An open space so that if you accidently drop the bell, it won't cause any serious structural damage.

The Workout:

You will have to repeat the circuit 4 to 5 times and workout at least 2 times a week; the optimum iterations per week would be 3 – 4. The exercises are as follows:

Double handed kettlebell swings – 15 reps:

The instructions are same as those given in the previous chapter.

Clean – 12 to 15 reps, each arm:

The whole idea of this particular exercise is to swiftly lift a kettlebell right in front of your shoulders and resting it at the top of your forearms. You can then perform either front squats or kettlebell presses. Note, that unlike its cousin, the barbell clean, the kettlebell clean is a prerequisite for many other exercises and not exactly a sufficient physical activity alone.

The activity however does target specific muscle groups that include glutes, hamstrings, lower back & core.

Start off by assuming the deadlift position, holding the kettlebell in between your legs with your right hand. The clean is a swift movement on its own and practically you should be executing a vertical jump on the spot but the kettlebell absorbs all this energy and channels it into something much more manageable.

Drive up the kettlebell but instead of having the arms fully extended, bend them a little so that the weight is closer to the body. This will also prevent the muscles in the arms from getting used up. Think of your arms as ropes that simply move the weights from one position to the next.

As soon as the kettlebell reaches the chest height, quickly tuck your arms underneath the bell so that the position comes to a halt and is locked.

Now you'll be in the racked or clean position. Notice how you're wrists are locked in straight and your forearms & hands are light.

Power tip – before you can master the clean technique, you must train on how to lower the kettlebell from the racked position. This can be done by placing the kettlebell in the rack position, maintaining the position with one arm and using the other arm to push the kettlebell over the holding hand. Finally, lowering the weight back to the deadlift position would do the trick. You'll have to repeat these steps a number of times to master it, but once you do, you'll have no problem executing the clean exercise.

Press – 12 to 15 reps, each arm:

The kettlebell press is a resilient exercise that trains the shoulders, laterals and biceps. To perform the exercise, you must first assume the rack position, as given above.

Start off in the rack position with your body tense, shoulders down and elbows tucked in. Have your laterals out wide and tighten your abdominal muscles so that your waist has adequate support to maintain the posture. Do not try to propel the kettlebell upwards by deriving power from your legs.

Right from the rack position, start rotating your shoulders outwards so that your forearms become vertical and the back of your load-bearing hand is behind you.

During a kettlebell press, the bell must follow a banana shaped arc when it gets lifted outwards and then up again. Similarly, remember to suck in your arms when you perform the lift in the vertical position, coming up next.

Finally, lift the kettlebell straight upwards, getting a full arm lockdown as you do so.

Here are some tips that will help you execute a better kettlebell press:

At the rack position, lower the shoulders as much as you can so that the muscles in and around the shoulders are properly stretched. This would allow these muscles to load up and attain better leverage; the elbows must make contact with the hipbones at the stretched position.

Flare out your back muscles (laterals) so that they diverge; this will allow the body to obtain greater stability, which will help with the vertical lift.

Take a hold of the handles as tight as possible, which will not only allow you to possess more control of the bell but will also help engage the arms while doing the lift.

While pressing the kettlebell concentrate on your shoulders & laterals and always derive power from these muscles and not the biceps.

Instead of thinking about actually lifting the bell, focus on driving yourself away from the kettlebell.

Russian twist – 8 reps, each side:

The exercise is fairly simple and requires the least amount of beforehand preparation.

Lie down on the ground while assuming the sit up position having a light kettlebell to your side.

Have your legs slightly bent.

Hold the kettlebell that rests by your side and pick it up.

Perform a twisting rotation so that the kettlebell ends at the other side of the body.

Go as far back as possible when performing the rotation, as long as you're not over extending your back.

Always be in control of the movement and carry it out slowly.

Push press – 12 to 15 reps, each side:

Begin the exercise while being in the push-up position; your body must positioned like a plank, facing the ground with both your arms making a vertical angle off the floor. But instead of having your hands rest on the floor, grab a pair of kettlebells and balance your weight on top of them.

Lower your body down while balancing on the kettlebells and bring your chest as close the ground as possible, then pushing away.

Once you reach the top position, lift a single kettlebell and balance your body weight on the one that rests. Stick your elbow behind your and have your wrist as close the abdomen as possible.

Lower the lifted weight back down into its original position and execute another lift, this time using the other shoulder.

Single leg RDL – 15 reps, each side:

Stand straight, having your feet at shoulder width and pick up a kettlebell with your right hand.

Start lifting your left leg behind you and as you do so, lower the rest of the body in the forward direction so balance is maintained.

Keep lowering yourself to a comfortable position until the kettlebell just touches the ground, and then lift yourself backup.

Windmills – 12 reps, each side:

The exercise is a great way to build up upper body strength; it targets laterals, oblique, core and shoulders. It is more of a support exercise and the best way to learn this exercise is by starting out with smaller weights.

Stand shoulder width apart and have your toes pointing outwards.

Grab the kettlebell with your right hand and raise it vertically upwards; keep lifting until the arm locks and kick the left hip out so you don't tip yourself off. The left hand should be doing nothing and set loose.

Breathe in and hold your abdominal muscles tight as you make the vertical lift; this will prevent any sudden jerk from damaging your back.

Look to the kettlebell and bend it towards the left hip; now move your left hand and place it against your left thigh. As you move the kettlebell downwards, you may bend the left leg a little but remember that the leg must always be locked.

Continue to bend your hips and slide your left hand down the thigh and the lower leg until you reach the ground. If you do not possess this amount of flexibility then just lower it down as much as possible. With time your flexibility will increase and you'll be able to execute this properly.

Now squeeze your glutes and move all the way up.

Repeat with the other hand.

If you're facing too much difficulty while successfully executing this exercise then try it without any added weight until you reach optimum flexibility.

When performing the exercise make sure that you never bend backwards. Also, it is vital that you are in control throughout the exercise; a number of people have damaged their oblique muscles while vertically lifting the kettlebell, then dropped the kettlebell on their heads and made the injury worse.

The Routine:

The following routine packs a full week's workout; your aim should be to repeat the circuit 3 times in a week, for six weeks. The tables will act as a guideline and help you track your performance at the end of each week.

When performing the exercises, aim for minimal reps so that you'll be able to catch your breath from time to time. You are allowed to rest 1 - 2 minutes between each round but you don't need to execute all 6 rounds, 3 – 4 would do just fine.

Complete as many rounds as possible within 20 minutes.

Begin and end each circuit with 5 minutes of treadmill or stationary bike.

Monday's Workout							
	Weight	Rd.1	Rd.2	Rd.3	Rd.4	Rd.5	Rd.6
Double kettlebell swing							
Clean							
Press							
Russian							

twist						
Push press						
Single leg RDL						
Windmills						

Wednesday's Workout							
	Weight	Rd.1	Rd.2	Rd.3	Rd.4	Rd.5	Rd.6
Double kettlebell swing							
Clean							
Press							
Russian twist							
Push							

press						
Single leg RDL						
Windmills						

Friday's Workout

	Weight	Rd.1	Rd.2	Rd.3	Rd.4	Rd.5	Rd.6
Double kettlebell swing							
Clean							
Press							
Russian twist							
Push press							
Single							

leg RDL							
Windmills							

Chapter 11: Beginner Kettlebell Workouts.

Workout 1A - The Newbie

"In the beginner's mind there are many possibilities, but in the expert's there are few" - Shunryu Suzuki

If you have never used Kettlebells before I strongly suggest you do only this workout for the first couple of weeks while you get used to swinging the Kettlebell.

It's a nice easy workout that is designed to get you into Kettlebells slowly and help you get the functional movements down without

Time: 10 minutes (Split into 1 minute rounds)

Exercises: Two Handed Kettlebell Swing

Set a timer for 1 minute rounds and each minute you need to do 10 swings. If you feel any pain or discomfort end the workout immediately.

Minute 1: 10 two-handed swings

Minute 2: 10 two-handed swings

Minute 3: 10 two-handed swings

Minute 4: 10 two-handed swings

Minute 5: 10 swings

Minute 6: 10 swings

And so on until you have done 10 minutes (and 100 swings).

Workout 1B - The Bilbo Baggins

"It's a dangerous business, Frodo, going out of your door" - Bilbo Baggins

Yes stay in and do this Kettlebell workout instead. Much safer! This is where I begin to challenge you with the workouts and make you exhale a little (or a lot depending on your fitness level). But don't worry I haven't made it too difficult.

Time: 10 minutes (Split into 1 minute rounds)

Exercises: Two Handed Kettlebell Swing

Set a timer for 1 minute rounds and each minute you need to do the required number of swings. Once you have finished rest for the remainder of the round. If you feel any pain or discomfort end the workout immediately.

Minute 1: 20 two-handed swings

Minute 2: 20 two-handed swings

Minute 3: 20 two-handed swings

Minute 4: 20 two-handed swings

Minute 5: 20 two-handed swings

Minute 6: 20 two-handed swings

And so on until you have done the whole 10 minutes. You should have about 20-30 seconds rest between rounds after finishing your 20 swings. The quicker you get your 20 swings done the more rest you will get between rounds. Do not rush the exercises make sure to maintain proper form at all costs.

Workout 1C - The Jesse Pinkman

"This is my own private domicile and I will not be harassed...bitch" - Jesse Pinkman

Why go to a gym and be harassed by Personal Trainers? Stay home and get in shape instead. Gatorade me bitch!

Time: 10 minutes (Split into 1 minute rounds)

Exercises: Two Handed Kettlebell Swing

This is where the workouts start to get a little more challenging. By minute 5 you should be breathing heavy and by minute 9 you should be feeling tired.

Minute 1: 30 two-handed swings

Minute 2: 30 two-handed swings

Minute 3: 30 two-handed swings

Minute 4: 30 two-handed swings

Minute 5: 30 two-handed swings

Minute 6: 30 two-handed swings

And so on until you have done the whole 10 minutes. You should have about 20-30 seconds rest between rounds. As the workouts are picking up intensity it is really important to do 30 air squats to warm up and then some more to warm down at the end of the workout.

Intermediate Kettlebell Workouts.

Workout 2A - The Batman

"You either die a hero or live long enough to see yourself become the villain. " - Bruce Wayne

Stay in and do some kettlebells instead then you'll always be a hero.

Time: About 10 minutes

Exercises: Two Handed Kettlebell Swing, Kettlebell Squat

If you feel any pain or discomfort end the workout immediately.

20 Two Handed Kettlebell Swings

20 Kettlebell Squats

20 Two Handed Kettlebell Swings

20 Kettlebell Squats

20 Two Handed Kettlebell Swings

20 Kettlebell Squats

20 Two Handed Kettlebell Swings

20 Kettlebell Squats

20 Two Handed Kettlebell Swings

20 Kettlebell Squats

20 Two Handed Kettlebell Swings

20 Kettlebell Squats

Try to do the entire workout without resting. It will be hard if you need to have a rest take one, but try and get as far through the workout as you can before needing one. By the time you have finished you will have done 200 reps. Congratulate yourself. Make sure to always use proper form. Remember Batman always uses proper form! Workout 2B - The Good, The Bad and The Ugly

"You see, in this world there's two kinds of people, my friend: Those with loaded guns and those who dig. You dig." - Blondie (1966)

Actually there's two kinds of people: those that swing and those who don't. You are a swinger. NO not that kind!!

Time: About 12 minutes

Exercises: Two Handed Kettlebell Swing, One Handed Kettlebell Swing

This is going to be the hardest workout so far

20 Two Handed Kettlebell Swings

10 Left-Hand Kettlebell Swings

10 Right-Hand Kettlebell Swings

20 Two Handed Kettlebell Swings

10 Left-Hand Kettlebell Swings

10 Right-Hand Kettlebell Swings

20 Two Handed Kettlebell Swings

10 Left-Hand Kettlebell Swings

10 Right-Hand Kettlebell Swings

20 Two Handed Kettlebell Swings

10 Left-Hand Kettlebell Swings

10 Right-Hand Kettlebell Swings

20 Two Handed Kettlebell Swings

10 Left-Hand Kettlebell Swings

10 Right-Hand Kettlebell Swings

So by the end you will have done 5 sets of 20 two-handed swings and 20 single handed swings (10 left and 10 right). 200 swings in total for the entire workout. Try and do as much of the workout as you can without resting. If you form starts to deteriorate make sure you rest for a minute or two.

Workout 2C - The Sterling Archer

"Call Kenny Loggins cause you're in the Danger Zone!" - Sterling Archer

All I've had today, is like six gummy bears and some scotch.

Time: About 10 minutes

Exercises: Two Handed Kettlebell Swing, Kettlebell Squat

If you feel any pain or discomfort end the workout immediately.

30 Two Handed Kettlebell Swings

20 Kettlebell Squats

30 Two Handed Kettlebell Swings

20 Kettlebell Squats

30 Two Handed Kettlebell Swings

20 Kettlebell Squats

30 Two Handed Kettlebell Swings

20 Kettlebell Squats

30 Two Handed Kettlebell Swings

20 Kettlebell Squats

30 Two Handed Kettlebell Swings

20 Kettlebell Squats

Try to do the entire workout without resting. It will be hard if you need to have a rest take one, but try and get as far through the workout as you can before needing one. By the time you have finished you will have done 200 reps. Congratulate yourself. Make sure to always use proper form. Batman always uses proper form!

Chapter 12: Beginners, Intermediate And Advanced Level Kettlebell Workout Plan

Just as we mentioned earlier, it is critical that you engage in kettlebell exercises that your body can handle. This means that, if you are just getting started as a beginner, you are not supposed to engage in high-intensity kettlebell workouts. Here, we have three levels that will help guide how you engage in exercises that are suitable for your strength and level of flexibility to avoid unnecessary injuries.

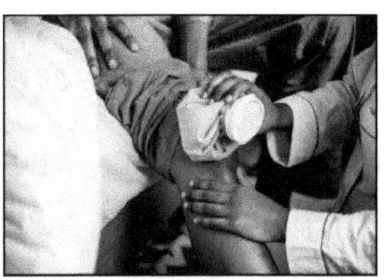

Beginner Level Kettlebell Workouts

The main objective of this is to increase your muscular strength as well as endurance in a large number of muscles in the body. It also plays a significant role in boosting the performance of your cardiovascular system. The total time recommended lies between 15 and 45 minutes. Additionally, the total number of circuits to be performed in a single workout should be three. This is laid out in the table below;

Kettlebell Exercises	Length of time	Important Notes
Kettlebell Swing	1-3 Minutes	One thing that you have to remember here is to drive your hips forward smoothly but with energy as you swing the kettlebell forward
Kettlebell Goblet	1-3	Here, it is critical that you squat as low as

Half Get Up	Minutes	you possibly can and then try to drive your hips back up through your heels
Kettlebell One-arm Row	1-3 Minutes	With this exercise, it is essential that you pull the kettlebells towards your tummy while ensuring that your spine maintains a straight posture (That is, the back straight and the chest out). Then keep your elbows tucked in
One-arm Overhead Press	1-3 Minutes	This is a great alternative to the common bench press we are familiar with. However, with the overhead press, it demands a compound

		wrist and movement of the arms
Kettlebell Halo	1-3 Minutes	As you exercise, one thing that you have to bear in mind is to
		keep your lower back in its natural arch and to the pivot

Intermediate Level Kettlebell Workouts

The main objective of this level of workout is to increase muscular strength and endurance. It is more difficult than the beginner level and can work the muscles three times as much. It also plays a critical role in boosting the performance of the cardiovascular system. The total amount of time taken here is estimated at 40 minutes. The total number of circuits to be performed at this level is three.

Kettlebell Exercises	Length of time/number of **repetitions**	Important Notes

Kettlebell Swing	12-15 minutes	Here, it is important that your glutes and hips drive the kettlebell forward instead of using your arms. The trick is to ensure that both the hips and the glutes are engaged throughout the exercise
KettlebellOne-arm Row	8-10 repetitions per side	Because you will have to do this for a couple of repetitions, it is important

		that you keep the spine at a neutral position throughout the exercise
One-armKettlebell Floor Press	8-10 repetitions per side	Remember to always turn your wrists towards the feet while pressing the kettlebell in the upward direction
Kettlebell Turkish Get Up	6-8 repetitions per side	This is quite a complex exercise that features a couple of movements. The most critical

		movement, in this case, is sliding the leg up in front of you so that it can offer you the support that you need while in a lunge position
Kettlebell Goblet Squat	12-15 minutes	Go as low as possible without allowing your tailbone to tuck under your butt.

Advanced Level Kettlebell Workouts

The advanced level of kettlebell workouts is suitable for those that have gone through the first two levels we have discussed and have attained a strong level of flexibility and muscular strength enough to handle the advanced workouts.

This level does not only promote muscular strength and endurance, but it also pays closer attention to strengthening the core and boosting the cardio capacity. The recommended length of time taken engaging in this level per session is 40 minutes while the total number of circuits to be performed per workout is three.

Kettlebell Exercises	Length of time/number of **repetitions**	Important Notes
Kettlebell Windmill	8-10 repetitions per side	Because this is a challenging exercise, it is advisable that you start with lightweight kettlebells at first. When you raise the kettlebell overhead, it is critical that you keep your eyes

		fixated on the weight so that you maintained proper shoulder alignment
Kettlebell Deadlift	Aim for at least 15 repetitions	Here, it is important that you engage the core, tighten the glutes and keep your arms as straight as possible when raising the body. The best way to achieve this is also to ensure that you push up your feet. Do not try to pull the kettlebells up using your arms. Instead, allow it to come naturally with you as you

		bring your body to a standing position

Kettlebell Clean	15-18 repetitions	While doing the kettlebell clean, remember that the grip position is important. As you begin, ensure that you keep your knees bent as you reach down to grip the handle of the kettlebell using your right hand. It is also important that you keep your thumb behind you. While in a rack

		position, the kettlebell should rest on your forearm tucked closer to your body while your fist is held at the chest level
Kettlebell Split Jerk	4-5 per leg at first and gradually build it up to 8-10 as your fitnesslevel increases	If you are going to do this right, it is advisable that you master the clean and the overhead press first which form the most critical stages of this complex workout
Kettlebell Pistol Squat	4-5 per leg at first and gradually build it up to 8-10 as your	When going up to a standing position, ensure that you drive up using your heels

| | fitnesslevel increases | |

Conclusion

The amazing kettlebell has been around for centuries. While no one is able to pinpoint its exact origin, no one can deny the extreme benefits it has had for the fitness industry. Athletes and laypeople have been using it diligently for their workout routines and they have been amazed by the results. Top level athletes from many different sports, including myself, now swear by this piece of exercise equipment and we have replaced many other workout routines for it. We have not been disappointed yet.

I have provided detailed descriptions of the kettlebell and the value that each type will bring. I also included some of the negative aspects of each type so that you can make the most informed decision possible. In the end, the two highest quality types are the cast-iron and competition kettlebells. These will provide you with all of the workouts you will need, especially when used in combination. Whatever type of kettlebell you end up getting, do not sacrifice quality for price. This will be an investment and if you choose wisely, a kettlebell will last you for years and maybe even a lifetime.

Definitely consider your own comfort level too. My hope is that the information I provided in the chapters will help you decide which one is right for you. Do your research and make your decision wisely. A poor choice here can cause a lot of pain and frustration in the long run.

The kettlebell provides many benefits. The workouts you will receive are tremendous and will target every major area of the body. The results you witness will be like nothing you have ever seen before. The major benefits include, but are not limited to, strength and cardio elevation, increased power and balance, better mobility and coordination, improved ability to perform regular activities of daily living, increased muscle mass, and improved overall health and wellness.

One of the greatest benefits, especially with our busy lives, is the convenience. The kettlebell can be stored almost anywhere in the house and when needed, just take it out and get to work. Since the workouts are intense and target multiple areas at once, you don't have to spend a lot of time doing them. 20-30 minutes a few times a week is plenty. You will have to go to the gym and spend several hours using various equipment to get the same results. With the kettlebell, it is all within the comfort of your own home.

Before using a kettlebell, become familiar with it and even perform some of the movements required without a kettlebell first. This will ensure you get the most out of your workouts and also maintain your safety. When you are ready to roll, start performing the many workouts I have provided. These training sessions are diverse and will help introduce the kettlebell into your life. Once you get familiar with it, you can add many others. always remember that form is much more important than speed or the number of reps. Once you get the proper movements down, then you can increase the amount and intensity level of the workouts. Take it slow and don't go any faster than you need to.

While you will be hard-pressed to find workouts that beat the kettlebell training, there are certainly some exercises that can complement it. While you don't need to incorporate these if you choose not to, you certainly don't have to dismiss them either. For example, things like pushups can enhance muscle building workouts and crunches can certainly add to the core training workouts. Whatever you do, make the kettlebell the central part of your routine.

I have also provided some information on supplements and nutrition. It is imperative that you are careful about what you put inside your body. The supplements that were discussed in chapter six will enhance your workouts in a major way and significantly add to your positive results.

They are essential for proper healing and functioning of your muscles and other body systems. Also, do not forget about your diet. Nutrition is important because we need the right fuel to drive out various metabolic processes. Intake of the proper nutrients will also add to our workouts.

Taking in the right supplements and nutrition will help ensure we have a proper recovery, reduced pain and injury, and better performance overall. Before starting the kettlebell training, consider your diet and supplement intake so you can get the most out of what I discussed today. My goal is to make sure you get healthy, shredded, and remain safe with high-level kettlebell circuits.

Your next step is to take the information you obtained in this book and begin utilizing it in your own life. Start taking massive action to improve your fitness and health. In the end, action is what creates results.

www.ingramcontent.com/pod-product-compliance
Lightning Source LLC
LaVergne TN
LVHW011949070526
838202LV00054B/4859